WARRIORS OF HISTORY

NINJA

by Jason Glaser & Don Roley

Consultant:
Don Roley
Ninjutsu Research Specialist
Ryugasaki, Japan

Mankato, Minnesota

Edge Books are published by Capstone Press,
151 Good Counsel Drive, P.O. Box 669, Mankato, Minnesota 56002.
www.capstonepress.com

Library of Congress Cataloging-in-Publication Data
Glaser, Jason.
    Ninja / by Jason Glaser and Don Roley.
    p. cm.—(Edge Books. Warriors of History)
    Includes bibliographical references and index.
    ISBN-13: 978-0-7368-6432-9 (hardcover)
    ISBN-10: 0-7368-6432-6 (hardcover)
1. Ninjutsu. I. Title. II. Series.
GV1114.73G53 2007
355.5'48—dc22   2005034933

Summary: Describes Ninja, including their history, weapons, and way of life.

Editorial Credits
Mandy Robbins, editor; Thomas Emery, designer; Cynthia Martin, illustrator;
    Kim Brown, production artist; Jo Miller, photo researcher; Scott Thoms,
    photo editor

Photo Credits
Art Resource, NY/Erich Lessing, 12; Werner Forman, 5, 6–7
Capstone Press, 20–21; Karon Dubke, cover
Corbis/Asian Art & Archaeology, Inc., 26–27; Bruce Burkhardt, 28–29; Horace
    Bristol, 16; Ric Ergenbright, 24–25; Werner Forman, 13
Getty Images Inc./National Geographic/Justin Guariglia, 14; Time Life Pictures/
    Mansell, 10
The Granger Collection, New York, 9, 23

1 2 3 4 5 6 11 10 09 08 07 06

TABLE OF CONTENTS

CHAPTER 1

ORIGINS OF THE NINJA

Like the warriors themselves, the history of the ninja is surrounded by mystery. Most experts believe three groups of people helped create the ninja. These groups came together in neighboring areas of Japan called Iga and Koga.

The regions of Iga and Koga were close to the ancient capital city of Kyoto. Defeated warriors from battles near Kyoto hid in Iga and Koga to avoid capture.

Many immigrants from China and Korea lived in Iga and Koga as well. These immigrants brought with them new ideas about fighting.

LEARN ABOUT:
- *Birthplace of the ninja*
- *Government of ancient Japan*
- *Fighting for power*

Ninja were the top secret spies
of ancient Japan.

A popular legend teaches that the first ninja learned their skills from a demon called a tengu.

The rulers of the Todai temple in the city of Nara controlled much of Iga. Farmers in Iga paid taxes to the temple. But temple officials were greedy. High taxes drove the farmers to revolt many times.

When these warriors, immigrants, and farmers came together, they developed fighting skills later known as ninjutsu. By the late 15th century, those who practiced the art of ninjutsu were called ninja.

NINJA FOR HIRE

The government of ancient Japan was complicated. The emperor was the official ruler. But he was more of a religious leader than a government leader. Japan was really controlled by the shogun. The shogun was the general of the emperor's army. With the military under his control, the shogun had the most power.

If the shogun's power weakened, the country fell into confusion. Local rulers called daimyo fought to unite the country and replace the shogun.

Bit by bit, daimyo conquered parts of Japan, hoping to become the new ruler. Many daimyo hired ninja to help them fight.

Yoshinobu Tokugawa was Japan's last shogun.

9

CHAPTER II
WAY OF THE NINJA

LEARN ABOUT:
- *Secret missions*
- *Living in the shadows*
- *Growing up ninja*

Samurai warriors were the glorified heroes of Japan.

The samurai were Japan's warrior class. Most often, they were from wealthy families. Samurai considered themselves better than common people. They wanted glory in battle and honor in the eyes of others. When seeking out spies, the daimyo would use ninja instead of samurai. Ninja were willing to pose as common people.

Ninja carried out secret missions. They lived quiet lives, slyly gathering information. Ninja mapped out territory while going about their daily business. They convinced members of the enemy's army to betray him. Then, ninja waited patiently for the proper time to act.

Because their identities were secret, ninja were greatly feared. A daimyo could never be certain he didn't have a ninja living in his midst. Ninja lived in the shadows, fought in the shadows, and died in the shadows. Those who became famous were considered failures.

THE LIFE OF A NINJA

Ninja began teaching ninjutsu to their children at an early age. Children learned to balance, jump, hide, and run through mazes. Later, they learned how to fight with their hands and feet. As teenagers, ninja trained with weapons and learned to spy on enemies.

In the hands of a ninja, an ordinary hand-held fan could be deadly.

A ninja might spend years posing as a monk while secretly gathering information.

To hide their identities, many ninja lived most of their lives in disguise. They worked as merchants, traveling from place to place. They posed as monks going on religious trips. Some ninja even worked as wandering samurai called ronin. These disguises gave them excuses to travel. They visited places where they could gather information and prepare sneak attacks.

While ninja were somctimes hired to kill, it was not common. Still, ninja became more feared as hired killers than as spies. The ninja's ability to sneak into places frightened people. In many cases, ninja sneaked into heavily armed camps and set fires. Sometimes, the rumor that enemy ninja were in camp caused more trouble than the ninja themselves.

EDGE FACT

Most ninja were men, but there were also female ninja called kunoichi.

CHAPTER III

TOOLS OF THE NINJA

LEARN ABOUT:
- *Ninja clothing*
- *Hidden weapons*
- *Walking on water*

Many people think of ninja as men dressed in black. People practicing ninjutsu today may wear black for training. But true ninja did not wear black on missions. The black outfit was used in Japanese theater. It was worn by stagehands working in the background. Like the stagehands, ninja seemed to blend into the background. People imagined ninja wore black too.

On field missions, ninja usually wore dark outfits of blue, green, rust, or brown. These colors blended well into many backgrounds. The clothes were sewn in familiar patterns of the times. But the ninja sewed secret pockets in their clothes to hide tools and weapons. Sometimes, ninja hid their faces with masks.

Wearing a mask was the perfect way to hide a ninja's identity.

Ninja chose their outfits by studying nature and learning what colors looked natural in shadows.

Hoods:
Hoods were used to conceal a ninja's identity.

Secret pockets:
Pockets could be sewn anywhere on a ninja's outfit to hold tools.

Belt:
A ninja could use his belt to help him climb buildings and trees.

Shoes:
Depending on the situation, ninja wore sandals, spikes, or small rafts on their feet.

SECRET WEAPONS

The ninja's weapons and tools had to be
easily hidden. Ninja often used a short sword
that could be hidden in small places. Some ninja
hollowed out canes to hold swords and knives.
Chains were balled up into the hand. Poisons and
powders were tucked away in pouches. Kunoichi
sometimes hid weapons in flowers, in their hair,
or in their pets' hair.

Ninja also used common objects as deadly
weapons. Walking sticks, canes, thin ropes, and
digging tools could all be used in a fight. Ninja
disguised as fishers or butchers could carry
knives without drawing suspicion.

To enter a place secretly, ninja often attached
steel claws to their hands and feet. These claws
helped them climb walls and trees. They could
also be used as weapons. The claws on a hand
could block or catch a swinging sword.

Ninja were masters of using fire as a weapon. A common ninja mission was sneaking into an enemy castle and setting it on fire. When guns were introduced to Japan, ninja were eager to use the new fire-powered weapons as well.

COVERING THEIR TRACKS

To keep their identities secret, ninja ran away if they were attacked. They used special tools to help them. Ninja used powder to distract and blind the enemy. To stop enemies from chasing them, ninja threw star-shaped blades called shaken behind them. They also dropped sharp spikes on the ground.

Checkpoints for catching spies were set up at bridges. To avoid checkpoints, ninja crossed rivers wearing small rafts or clay pots on their feet. The odd footwear allowed ninja to float on the water.

Ninja throwing stars called shaken came in many star and diamond shapes.

Ninja hid their identities at home too. Weapons and tools were hidden in secret panels or under floorboards. Hidden ladders and tunnels made it possible to sneak in and out of the house. A well-designed home could even have a secret room hidden in the center.

CHAPTER IV

THE NINJA FADE AWAY

In the late 1500s, a powerful daimyo named Nobunaga Oda began conquering Japan. He allowed Christian missionaries from Europe into the country. These missionaries were often former military men. They taught Oda much of what they knew. Oda soon began using guns and long spears, like Europeans did.

Though Oda had become very powerful, some areas were not under his control. One such place was the Iga region. The ninja there had thrown out the daimyo and ruled themselves. They worked for daimyo from other regions, as long as these rulers promised not to attack Iga.

LEARN ABOUT:
- Nobunaga Oda
- Ninja protectors
- The Tokugawa reign

Nobunaga Oda was a strong daimyo who wanted to destroy the ninja of Iga.

In 1579, Oda's son and his best samurai warriors attacked Iga. Although they were greatly outnumbered, the ninja of Iga stopped the attack. Furious, Oda ordered thousands of troops to attack again in 1581. This time, the ninja were overrun and fled. Many daimyo around Iga took ninja into their homes and hired them.

Statues of Ieyasu Tokugawa still stand today to honor the Japanese leader.

AN EMPIRE IN CHAOS

In 1582, one of Oda's own men killed him. Oda's forces were left without a leader. A fight for power began among Oda's military. One man hungry for power was Ieyasu Tokugawa. He had taken in many of the Iga ninja. Now he needed them to repay his kindness.

Tokugawa was trapped far from his home.
He needed to get back to what is now Tokyo.
There, he could raise his own army. A ninja
named Hanzo Hattori offered to help Tokugawa.

Hattori arranged for ninja to protect
Tokugawa along his journey. Hattori and the
other ninja saved Tokugawa's life many times.

The Tokugawa family reigned for about 260 years and produced 15 shoguns.

A PEACEFUL NATION

Tokugawa went on to raise a strong army. By 1600, he had taken over all of Japan. The emperor made Tokugawa the shogun. Tokugawa always remembered what the ninja had done for him. He allowed them to live and train in peace.

The art of ninjutsu lives on through the teaching of modern-day martial arts.

The Tokugawa family ruled peacefully for about 260 years. With no fighting in Japan, ninja were not needed. The Tokugawa rulers used them as guards and assistants, but their skillful arts were rarely used. The ninja arts of war and stealth slowly faded away.

Today, martial arts schools teach skills of the early ninja. Many of these schools trace their teachings back to certain ninja groups. Even though students are taught ninjutsu, they don't live like the ninja of years ago. Those mysterious warriors live only in the stories of the past.

GLOSSARY

daimyo (DIME-yo)—a feudal lord of Japan who was a large landowner

ninjutsu (nihn-JIHT-soo)—skills practiced by a ninja

samurai (SAH-muh-rye)—a skilled Japanese warrior who served one master or leader

shogun (SHOH-gun)—a Japanese warlord who was in charge of the emperor's armies

stealth (STELTH)—the ability to remain undetected by others

READ MORE

Chaline, Eric. *Ninjutsu.* Martial and Fighting Arts. Broomall, Penn.: Mason Crest Publishers, 2003.

Collins, Paul. *Ninjutsu.* Martial Arts. Broomall, Penn.: Chelsea House, 2002.

Mattern, Joanne. *Ninjas: Masters of Stealth and Secrecy.* Way of the Warrior. New York: Rosen, 2005.

INTERNET SITES

FactHound offers a safe, fun way to find Internet sites related to this book. All of the sites on FactHound have been researched by our staff.

Here's how:
1. Visit *www.facthound.com*
2. Choose your grade level.
3. Type in this book ID **0736864326** for age-appropriate sites. You may also browse subjects by clicking on letters, or by clicking on pictures and words.
4. Click on the **Fetch It** button.

FactHound will fetch the best sites for you!

INDEX